Great Inventions

THE LIGHT BULB

by Marc Tyler Nobleman

Consultant:
Hal Wallace
Historian, Electricity Collections
National Museum of American History
Smithsonian Institution, Washington, D.C.

Capstone
press

Mankato, Minnesota

Fact Finders is published by Capstone Press,
151 Good Counsel Drive, P.O. Box 669, Mankato, Minnesota 56002.
www.capstonepress.com

Library of Congress Cataloging-in-Publication Data
Nobleman, Marc Tyler.
    The light bulb / Marc Tyler Nobleman.
    p. cm.—(Fact finders. Great inventions)
    Includes bibliographical references (p. 31) and index.
    Contents: A better light—Before the light bulb—Inventors—How a light bulb works—
Lighting the world—Light bulbs today.
    ISBN 0-7368-2216-X (hardcover)
    ISBN 0-7368-4541-0 (paperback)
    1. Light bulbs—Juvenile literature. [1. Light bulbs.] I. Title. II. Series.
TK4351.N63 2004
621.32′6—dc21   2002156501

Editorial Credits

Roberta Schmidt, editor; Juliette Peters, series designer and illustrator; Alta Schaffer,
    photo researcher; Eric Kudalis, product planning editor

Photo Credits

Capstone Press/Gary Sundermeyer, 1, 27 (right)
Corbis/Royalty Free, cover, 26 (right); The Bettmann Archive, 8
Digital Vision Ltd., 24–25
Hulton/Archive Photos by Getty Images, 5, 9, 13, 14 (both), 15, 19, 23
Image Library, 27 (left)
North Wind Picture Archives, 6–7
Philips Lighting Company, 27 (middle)
Schenectady Museum, 20–21, 22
Smithsonian Institution, neg. #43,893a, 10–11; neg. #79_9516t, 26 (middle)
Stock Montage Inc., 26 (left)

2 3 4 5 6 08 07 06 05 04

Table of Contents

Chapter 1

A Better Light

In 1879, Thomas Edison and his helpers were working hard in Edison's workshop. Edison was trying to make a light bulb. Many other people had tried and failed. Some scientists did not think a light bulb was possible.

Edison and his workers were trying to find a material that would work in the light bulb. The material had to glow as electricity went through it. It had to burn for a long time. It also had to glow brightly. The men tested hundreds of materials.

In late October, one of Edison's lamps glowed for more than 13 hours. It burned longer than any other lamp. The light bulb was born.

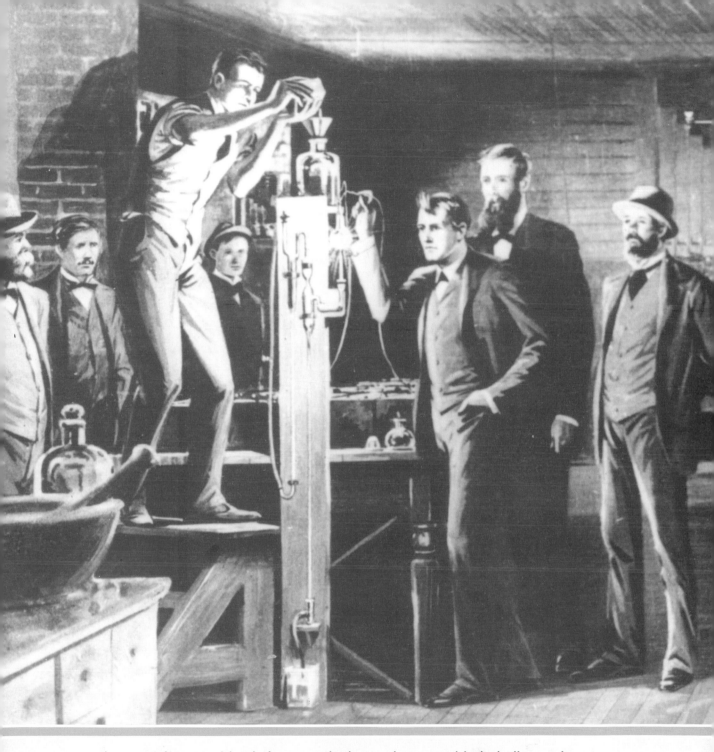

Thomas Edison and his helpers worked to make a good light bulb at Edison's laboratory in Menlo Park, New Jersey.

Chapter 2

Before the Light Bulb

For hundreds of years, people looked for a cheap and easy light source. They wanted to be able to see after the Sun set. Before the light bulb, people had to use fireplaces, candles, or gas or oil lamps for light.

Candles and Oil Lamps

Candles and oil lamps cost a lot and were dirty. Candles made from animal fat filled homes with smoke and soot. Lamps using fish or vegetable oil also were smoky and dirty.

Before the light bulb, some people used fireplaces for light.

Some people burned whale oil in their lamps. Whale oil was not as dirty as vegetable or fish oil. But whale oil cost a lot of money. Many people did not have enough money to buy it.

Oil lamps and candles needed a lot of care. People worked hard to keep their homes lit. People who used a lamp had to clean it every day. They also had to trim the lamp wick.

Oil lamps have open flames and can be dangerous.

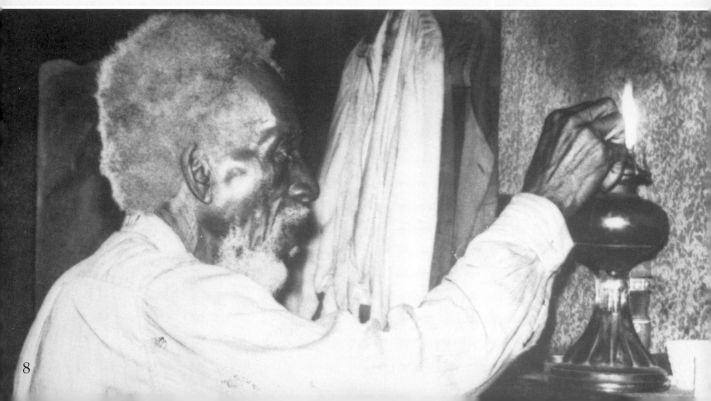

Candles burned down quickly. People who used candles had to buy new candles often or make their own.

Candles and lamps could be dangerous. They have open flames. Open flames can easily cause fires. People needed to be careful not to let anything touch the flame.

Gas Lamps

In the early 1800s, people began to use gas lamps. These lamps burned a gas made from coal or wood. Later, gas lamps burned natural gas.

Gas lamps were not as dirty as other lamps, but they could be more dangerous. People sometimes forgot to turn off the gas after they blew out the flame. The gas would fill the house and make people sick. People could die from breathing in the gas.

Bright light from arc lamps lit city streets in the late 1800s.

Arc Lamps

In the late 1800s, some streets and public buildings were lit with arc lamps. These lamps used an arc of electric current to make light. Arc lamps were not used in people's homes. The light from arc lamps was too bright. The lamps also burned out quickly. People needed a light that was safe, cheap, and long-lasting.

The first arc lamp was made in 1807. It used a battery to create a 4-inch (10-centimeter) arc between two charcoal sticks.

Chapter 3

Inventors

In 1802, British chemist Sir Humphrey Davy made an important discovery. He found that running electricity through a material could make it glow brightly for a few seconds before burning up. Davy's discovery was called electrical incandescence. It made the invention of the light bulb possible.

Sir Humphrey Davy was a British chemist.

Joseph Swan

In early 1879, Sir Joseph Swan built a working light bulb. But his light bulb had problems. The carbon burning inside the bulb slowly turned the glass black. The wires in the bulb melted when they got too hot.

Joseph Swan was a British chemist and physicist.

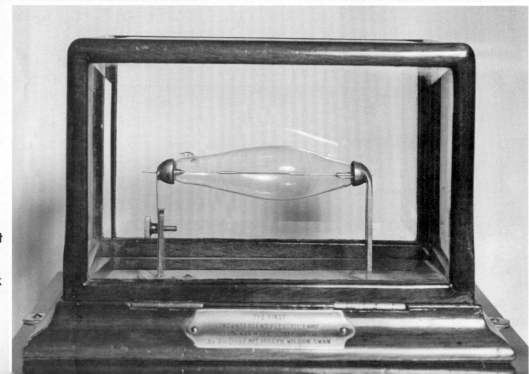

Swan's incandescent light bulb did not work very well.

Thomas Edison

Like Swan, Edison wanted to make a long-lasting light bulb. He worked with many different types of materials. He tried to find the material that would glow brightest and longest.

In October 1879, Edison had a breakthrough. He and his workers put a carbonized cotton thread in a light bulb. The baked thread glowed brightly in the bulb for more than 13 hours.

Edison also invented the phonograph, the movie projector, the automatic telegraph system, and many other machines.

Thomas Edison was an American inventor.

Chapter 4

How a Light Bulb Works

A light bulb has three main parts. It has a glass bulb, a metal base, and a filament. The glass bulb has no oxygen in it. Instead, today's bulbs are filled with different gases. These gases help the bulb give off more light than the Edison bulb.

The filament is the part of the light bulb that glows. Today's filaments are a thin piece of wire. The filament is held in the middle of the glass bulb by wires called lead-in wires. The lead-in wires run from the filament to the metal base of the light bulb.

Edison's light bulbs did not have any gases in them. Edison used a vacuum pump to suck the air out of the bulbs.

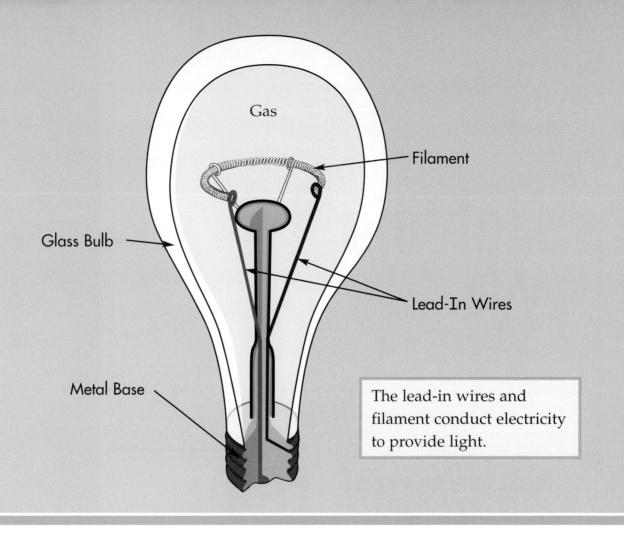

Gas

Filament

Glass Bulb

Lead-In Wires

Metal Base

The lead-in wires and filament conduct electricity to provide light.

A light bulb needs electricity. When the bulb is screwed into a light fixture, an electric current travels through the lead-in wires to the filament. The filament heats up and glows as the electric current passes through it.

Chapter 5

Lighting the World

On New Year's Eve 1879, more than 3,000 people went to Edison's workshop to see his invention. They were amazed. But several years passed before people had light bulbs in their homes.

The First Years

In the early 1880s, few people could use Edison's light bulbs. The light bulbs needed electricity to work. Most homes and businesses did not have electricity. Edison had to set up an electrical system to power his light bulbs.

People in the late 1800s were amazed by electric lights.

In 1882, Edison opened the Pearl Street Power Station in New York City. It was the nation's first central electrical power plant. The station made electricity and sold it to the public. Soon, hotels, theaters, and other businesses began to use Edison's lighting system.

Electric Lighting Becomes Popular

The electrical system let more people use light bulbs. People started to see that electric lighting was useful and easy. With light bulbs, they did not need to buy candles or fill oil lamps. Electric lighting became popular.

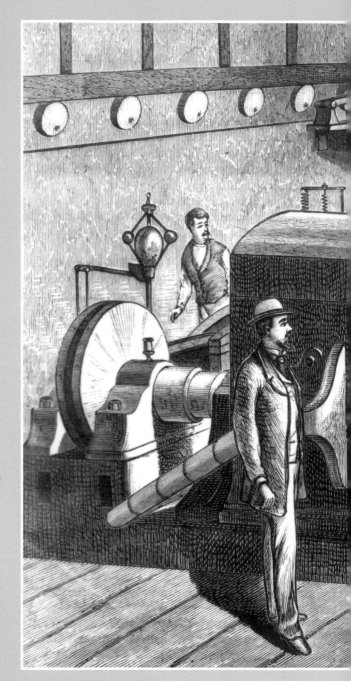

The Pearl Street Power Station produced electricity and sold it to the public.

William David Coolidge was an American engineer.

Improvements

Edison continued to work on the light bulb for many years. He searched for a better filament. He tried more than 6,000 materials from around the world. He even tried plants like hickory and cedar. He finally chose bamboo as the filament that worked best. By 1881, Edison had made a light bulb that burned for 600 hours.

In 1910, William David Coolidge helped to make the light bulb better. He invented a new type of filament made with tungsten. Tungsten is a metal that burns longer and brighter than other materials.

Tungsten filaments work at high temperatures. Most operate at 4,900° Fahrenheit (2,700° Celsius).

Coolidge's filament was stronger and easier to make than other filaments.

By 1920, many people had electric lights. But those who lived far from cities had to wait longer to get electrical wires. Some people had to wait until the 1950s for electric light.

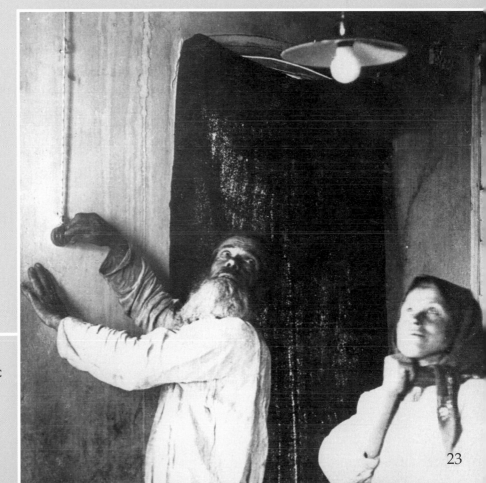

A couple switches on their first electric light in the 1920s.

Chapter 6

Light Bulbs Today

Electric lights have changed the world. Today, many types of light bulbs are used. The most common types are incandescent bulbs, halogen bulbs, and fluorescent bulbs.

Most homes use incandescent bulbs. These light bulbs are like the one Edison invented. They have a base that screws into light fixtures. Incandescent bulbs usually last about 1,000 hours.

Only 5 percent of the energy an incandescent light bulb uses makes light. The rest of the energy it uses makes heat.

Today, light bulbs light up large cities, such as Pittsburgh, Pennsylvania.

Halogen light bulbs are a brighter and hotter type of incandescent bulb. Halogen light bulbs have a tungsten filament. They are filled with halogen gas. Some people have halogen lamps in their homes. Halogen bulbs last 2,250 to 3,500 hours.

Fluorescent light bulbs are different from incandescent bulbs.

Light Bulbs through the Years

early tungsten
1913

Edison's bulb
1879

carbon filament
1900

Fluorescent bulbs make much less heat than incandescent bulbs. They also save energy. Fluorescent lights are often found in schools and offices. Some lamps also use fluorescent bulbs. These bulbs last 10,000 hours or more.

Light bulbs make light easy to use. They will continue to light homes and businesses for many years.

soft white
1950

krypton-filled
1970

tungsten-halogen
1990

Fast Facts

- **Arc lamps** produce bright light. They are still used today in some large spotlights.

- **Sir Humphrey Davy** discovered electrical incandescence in 1802.

- **Thomas Edison** made the first long-lasting light bulb in 1879. The light bulb used carbonized cotton for its filament and lasted more than 13 hours.

- In 1910, **William David Coolidge** invented a new and better filament made with tungsten.

- The amount of energy a light bulb uses is measured in **watts**.

- The amount of light a light bulb puts out is measured in **lumens**.

- The **bases** of Edison's light bulbs are the same size as today's light bulb bases. An Edison light bulb will screw into a modern light socket.

Hands On:

Light a Bulb

Flashlights and many toys have light bulbs that are powered by batteries. You can light up a light bulb by using a battery.

What You Need
an adult
tape
two 12-inch (30.5-centimeter) pieces of insulated copper wire
(Ask an adult to cut away the plastic on the wires at both ends so the bare wire is exposed.)
D-size battery
small (flashlight-size) light bulb

What You Do
1. Have an adult help you find the terminals on the light bulb and on the battery.
2. Tape one end of the first wire to the battery's bottom terminal.
3. Tape the other end of the same wire to one of the light bulb's terminals.
4. Tape one end of the second wire to the battery's top terminal.
5. Touch the other end of the wire to the light bulb's other terminal. The light bulb will light up.

Glossary

arc lamp (ARK LAMP)—a lamp that uses an arc of electric current between two electrodes to produce light

carbonize (KAR-buhn-ize)—to bake something to turn it into pure carbon

current (KUR-uhnt)—a flow of electric charge

filament (FIL-uh-muhnt)—a thin wire that is heated electrically to produce light

fluorescent (flu-RESS-uhnt)—giving out a bright light by using a certain type of energy; a fluorescent light turns light that people cannot see into a light that people can see.

incandescent (in-kan-DESS-uhnt)—glowing with strong light and heat

invention (in-VEN-shuhn)—a new thing

inventor (in-VEN-tuhr)—a person who makes something new

Internet Sites

Do you want to find out more about Edison and the light bulb?
Let FactHound, our fact-finding hound dog, do the research for you.

Here's how:
1) Visit *http://www.facthound.com*
2) Type in the **Book ID** number:
   073682216X
3) Click on **FETCH IT**.

FactHound will fetch Internet sites picked by our editors just for you!

Read More

Evans, Neville. *The Science of a Light Bulb.* Science World. Austin, Texas: Raintree Steck-Vaughn, 2000.

Tagliaferro, Linda. *Thomas Edison: Inventor of the Age of Electricity.* Minneapolis: Lerner Publications, 2003.

Wallace, Joseph. *The Lightbulb.* Turning Point Inventions. New York: Atheneum Books for Young Readers, 1999.

Index